Reclaiming Time

Reclaiming Time

Matthew Petchinsky

Reclaiming Time: How to Live More by Doing Less
By: Matthew Petchinsky

Introduction

In the hustle and bustle of modern life, time has become a luxury that many of us can scarcely afford. The world is moving faster than ever, with technology and societal expectations constantly demanding our attention. It's no wonder that we often feel stretched thin, overwhelmed, and disconnected from the things that truly matter. Yet, amidst the chaos, there exists a timeless truth: simplifying our lives can lead to profound meaning and fulfillment.

Why Modern Life Steals Your Time

At first glance, modern advancements seem to promise convenience and efficiency. Smartphones, smart homes, and countless apps are marketed as tools to save time and make life easier. But as these technologies integrate into our daily lives, they often have the opposite effect. Notifications, emails, and endless streams of content pull us in a hundred different directions. Our schedules are packed with commitments, leaving little room for reflection, rest, or genuine connection.

Consider how much of your day is consumed by distractions. Social media platforms are designed to capture and hold your attention, turning minutes into hours without you even realizing it. Work demands have also skyrocketed, with many of us tethered to our devices even after official working hours. The line between personal time and professional obligations has blurred, creating a constant sense of urgency. This relentless pace not only steals your time but also erodes your mental clarity and emotional well-being.

Moreover, societal pressures often push us to equate busyness with success. We are encouraged to chase material possessions, professional milestones, and social approval, believing these will lead to happiness. Instead, they often lead to exhaustion, as we scramble to meet expectations that are neither sustainable nor deeply fulfilling.

The paradox of modern life is this: while we have more tools to save time than ever before, we are losing our ability to truly enjoy the time we have.

The Art of Simplifying for More Meaningful Living

Simplifying your life is not about giving up everything you love or retreating from the world. Instead, it's about intentionally choosing what deserves your energy and focus. It's about curating a life that aligns with your values, where time is spent on things that bring joy, growth, and connection.

The art of simplifying begins with awareness. By understanding where your time goes and identifying the areas of your life that feel cluttered—physically, emotionally, or mentally—you can start to reclaim control. This process might involve decluttering your home, streamlining your schedule, or even re-evaluating relationships that drain rather than nourish you.

Simplifying also means embracing the power of saying "no." Many of us overcommit, fearing disappointment or conflict, but every "yes" to something unimportant is a "no" to something that truly matters. By setting boundaries and prioritizing what aligns with your deepest desires, you create space for the things that enrich your life.

At its core, simplifying is about shifting your mindset. It's a commitment to live intentionally rather than reactively, to focus on quality over quantity, and to seek depth rather than breadth in your experiences. It's recognizing that life is finite and choosing to invest your time and energy wisely.

In this book, we'll explore practical strategies to help you simplify your life and reclaim your time. From managing digital distractions to fostering mindfulness, each chapter will guide you toward a more meaningful and intentional way of living. By the end, you'll have the tools to design a life that feels not only productive but also fulfilling—a life where you can breathe deeply, connect genuinely, and find joy in the present moment.

As you embark on this journey, remember that simplicity isn't a destination but a practice. It's an ongoing effort to align your daily actions with your true values and desires. The reward? A life rich in meaning, where every moment feels purposeful and time becomes your ally rather than your enemy.

Chapter 1: The Time Audit

Time is the most valuable resource we have, yet it often slips through our fingers without us even realizing it. Before we can reclaim our time, we must understand where it is going. The time audit is a powerful tool to uncover the truth about how you spend your days and help you make meaningful changes. By identifying hidden time drains and learning to prioritize effectively, you can take control of your schedule and live a more intentional life.

Identifying Where Your Time Really Goes

The first step in a time audit is awareness. Most people have only a vague idea of how they spend their time, often underestimating how much is consumed by distractions, multitasking, or low-priority activities. To gain clarity, it's essential to analyze your day in detail.

Step 1: Track Your Time

Begin by documenting your daily activities for a week. Use a journal, spreadsheet, or time-tracking app to record everything you do, from work tasks to leisure activities. Break your day into small increments—15 or 30 minutes—to capture a clear picture of how your time is distributed.

Be honest and specific. Instead of writing "work," note the specific tasks you performed, such as "answered emails," "attended a meeting," or "brainstormed project ideas." Similarly, replace vague entries like "relaxed" with more precise activities, such as "watched TV," "read a book," or "scrolled social media."

Step 2: Categorize Your Activities

Once you've collected your data, categorize your activities into broad groups. Common categories include:

- **Work:** Tasks and responsibilities related to your job or career.
- **Personal Development:** Activities like exercising, reading, or learning a new skill.
- **Social:** Time spent with family, friends, or in social settings.
- **Leisure:** Entertainment, hobbies, or relaxation.
- **Necessities:** Essential activities like eating, commuting, and sleeping.

As you categorize, note whether each activity was productive, neutral, or unproductive. This helps you identify patterns and areas for improvement.

Step 3: Analyze Your Patterns

With your data categorized, look for trends:

- Are you spending more time on low-value activities than you realized?
- Are there specific times of day when you're more prone to distractions?
- Are your priorities aligned with how you spend your time?

For example, if you value personal growth but spend only an hour a week on it while dedicating 10 hours to social media, there's a misalignment. Recognizing these discrepancies is the first step toward change.

Tools to Analyze and Reprioritize

After identifying how your time is spent, the next step is to make adjustments. Several tools and techniques can help you analyze your data and create a more balanced, intentional schedule.

The Eisenhower Matrix

The Eisenhower Matrix, also known as the Urgent-Important Matrix, helps you categorize tasks based on their urgency and importance:

- **Important and Urgent:** Tasks that require immediate attention. Handle these first.
- **Important but Not Urgent:** High-value tasks that contribute to long-term goals. Schedule these.
- **Urgent but Not Important:** Tasks that demand attention but don't add significant value. Delegate or minimize these.
- **Not Urgent and Not Important:** Low-value activities that waste time. Eliminate these.

Using the matrix, review your tracked activities and categorize them. This will help you identify tasks that deserve more focus and those that can be reduced or removed.

Pareto Principle (80/20 Rule)

The Pareto Principle states that 80% of outcomes come from 20% of efforts. Apply this principle by identifying the 20% of activities that yield the most significant results. For instance:

- Which work tasks drive the most impact?
- Which personal activities bring you the most joy or growth?

By focusing on these high-impact activities, you can maximize your results with less effort.

Time-Blocking

Time-blocking involves scheduling your day into specific blocks of time for different activities. This technique forces you to allocate time for priorities and minimizes the risk of wasting hours on unproductive tasks.

For example:

- 8:00–9:00 AM: Morning routine and personal development
- 9:00–12:00 PM: Focused work
- 12:00–1:00 PM: Lunch and relaxation
- 1:00–3:00 PM: Meetings or collaborative tasks
- 3:00–5:00 PM: Creative or strategic work
- 5:00–6:00 PM: Exercise and personal time

Review your time audit data to create a realistic schedule that aligns with your priorities.

Digital Tools and Apps

Several digital tools can streamline your time audit and prioritization process:

- **RescueTime:** Tracks your digital activity and provides insights into how you spend your time online.
- **Toggl Track:** A time-tracking app that allows you to categorize tasks and analyze productivity.
- **Google Calendar:** Use it for time-blocking and setting reminders.
- **Notion or Trello:** Organize tasks and goals with these project management tools.

Choose tools that suit your preferences and integrate seamlessly into your routine.

Reprioritizing Your Life

After completing your time audit and identifying areas for improvement, it's time to reprioritize. Ask yourself:

- What activities align with my values and long-term goals?
- What tasks can be delegated, automated, or eliminated?
- How can I create more time for what truly matters?

Reprioritization is not a one-time event but an ongoing process. Periodically repeat the time audit to ensure you stay aligned with your evolving goals.

Chapter 2: Cutting the Noise

Modern life is filled with distractions, obligations, and noise—both literal and metaphorical—that drain your energy and steal your focus. To reclaim your time and live more meaningfully, it's essential to cut through the clutter and eliminate the unnecessary. This chapter will guide you through identifying and eliminating low-value tasks and setting firm boundaries to protect your time and energy.

Eliminating Low-Value Tasks

Low-value tasks are the hidden culprits behind wasted time. These tasks often feel urgent but contribute little to your long-term goals or personal fulfillment. Recognizing and eliminating them is a critical step in simplifying your life.

Step 1: Identify Low-Value Tasks

Low-value tasks can vary from person to person, but common examples include:

- Excessive email checking
- Unnecessary meetings
- Endless scrolling on social media
- Overcommitting to obligations that don't align with your priorities
- Busywork that feels productive but achieves little

Use your time audit from Chapter 1 to identify which tasks fall into this category. Ask yourself:

- Does this task contribute to my goals or values?
- Could someone else handle this task more effectively?
- What would happen if I stopped doing this task entirely?

For instance, if you're spending an hour a day managing emails that don't require immediate attention, that time could be better spent on more meaningful activities.

Step 2: Prioritize High-Value Activities

Replacing low-value tasks with high-value activities is key to cutting the noise. High-value activities are those that:

- Move you closer to your long-term goals
- Provide significant returns on your time investment
- Enhance your well-being or bring you joy

Examples include focused work on critical projects, exercising, spending quality time with loved ones, and pursuing personal growth. Shift your focus toward these activities by scheduling them first in your day.

Step 3: Outsource, Automate, or Eliminate

For tasks that must be completed but don't require your personal attention, consider outsourcing or automating them. Here's how:

- **Outsource:** Delegate repetitive or time-consuming tasks to others. For instance, hire a virtual assistant to manage emails or a cleaning service to free up your weekends.
- **Automate:** Use tools and technology to streamline your workflow. Automate bill payments, set up email filters, and use apps to manage recurring tasks.
- **Eliminate:** For tasks that don't add value, give yourself permission to let them go. If attending a weekly meeting doesn't contribute to your work or goals, propose alternative solutions or opt out.

Eliminating low-value tasks frees up time and mental space, allowing you to focus on what truly matters.

Setting Boundaries for Your Time

Even when you've eliminated low-value tasks, your time can still be hijacked by external demands. Setting clear boundaries is essential for protecting your time and ensuring it's used intentionally.

Step 1: Define Your Priorities

Boundaries start with clarity about what's important to you. Reflect on your values, goals, and commitments. For example:

- How much time do you want to dedicate to work, family, self-care, and hobbies?
- What are your non-negotiables—activities or times that are sacred to you?

Once you've defined your priorities, you can create boundaries that support them.

Step 2: Learn to Say "No"

Saying "no" can be challenging, especially if you're used to pleasing others or fear conflict. However, every "yes" to something that doesn't align with your priorities is a "no" to something that does.

Practice saying "no" gracefully and assertively:

- **Be polite but firm:** "I really appreciate the offer, but I can't commit to that right now."
- **Offer alternatives:** "I'm not available to help with this, but I can recommend someone else who might be."
- **Set limits:** "I can join the meeting, but I'll need to leave after 30 minutes."

Remember, saying "no" is not selfish—it's a way to honor your time and energy.

Step 3: Establish Time Blocks

Protect your time by creating dedicated blocks for specific activities. For instance:

- Work in focused intervals without interruptions.
- Set aside "family time" or "me time" that's free from work or distractions.
- Reserve time for rest and reflection.

Communicate these boundaries clearly to others. Let colleagues know when you're unavailable for meetings or calls, and inform family members of your need for uninterrupted work or self-care time.

Step 4: Manage Digital Distractions

Technology is one of the biggest barriers to effective boundaries. Combat digital distractions with these strategies:

- **Turn off notifications:** Silence non-essential alerts on your phone and computer.
- **Limit screen time:** Use apps or settings to monitor and cap your time on social media or entertainment apps.
- **Create tech-free zones:** Designate areas or times of the day where devices are not allowed, such as during meals or before bedtime.

By controlling your digital environment, you can reclaim focus and minimize interruptions.

Step 5: Communicate Expectations

Setting boundaries is only effective if others respect them. Clearly communicate your expectations to colleagues, friends, and family:

- Let coworkers know when you're available for collaboration and when you need uninterrupted focus.
- Explain to friends or family why you're limiting certain activities and how they can support your goals.

Boundary-setting is a two-way street; be open to hearing and respecting others' boundaries as well.

Reclaiming Your Time and Energy

Cutting the noise from your life requires consistent effort and self-discipline. As you eliminate low-value tasks and set boundaries, you'll notice significant changes:

- More time for activities that align with your values
- Increased focus and productivity
- Greater sense of control over your schedule
- Improved relationships as you engage more fully in meaningful moments

Remember, the goal is not to cram more into your day but to create space for what truly matters. Cutting the noise allows you to live with intention, clarity, and purpose—free from the distractions and obligations that once held you back.

By mastering the art of eliminating the unnecessary and protecting your time, you'll be well on your way to a simpler, more fulfilling life. The next chapter will build on this foundation by exploring strategies for mindful living and intentional action.

Chapter 3: Designing Your Perfect Day

A perfect day isn't about perfection—it's about balance. It's about structuring your time in a way that aligns with your goals, values, and energy levels, creating space for productivity, rest, and joy. In this chapter, we'll explore how to design a daily schedule that promotes harmony, helps you achieve your goals, and leaves you feeling fulfilled.

Structuring Your Schedule for Balance

The key to designing your perfect day is intentionality. Without a plan, it's easy to drift through your day reacting to distractions and demands. A well-structured schedule provides clarity, reduces stress, and ensures that your time is spent meaningfully.

Step 1: Start with Your Priorities

Begin by identifying what truly matters to you. This will guide how you allocate your time. Consider these questions:

- What are your top three priorities for today, this week, or this month?
- Which activities bring you the most satisfaction and fulfillment?
- What tasks are essential to your personal and professional goals?

Write down your priorities and use them as the foundation for your schedule. For example, if your priorities include advancing a work project, exercising, and spending quality time with family, these should be the cornerstones of your day.

Step 2: Leverage Your Energy Cycles

Your energy levels naturally fluctuate throughout the day. Some people feel most productive in the morning, while others hit their stride in the afternoon or evening. Recognizing your energy patterns allows you to match tasks to your peak performance times:

- **High-energy periods:** Schedule focused, demanding tasks such as work projects, problem-solving, or creative endeavors.
- **Moderate-energy periods:** Reserve this time for routine tasks like responding to emails or organizing.
- **Low-energy periods:** Use this time for rest, reflection, or light activities like reading or taking a walk.

By aligning your tasks with your energy levels, you'll work more efficiently and reduce burnout.

Step 3: Create Time Blocks

Time-blocking is a powerful strategy for structuring your day. Divide your day into distinct blocks dedicated to specific types of activities. Here's an example of a balanced day:

- **Morning Block (7:00–9:00 AM):** Morning routine, exercise, and planning.
- **Focus Block (9:00–12:00 PM):** Deep work on high-priority tasks.
- **Midday Block (12:00–1:00 PM):** Lunch and relaxation.
- **Afternoon Block (1:00–4:00 PM):** Meetings, collaboration, or less demanding tasks.
- **Evening Block (4:00–6:00 PM):** Personal time, hobbies, or errands.
- **Night Block (6:00–9:00 PM):** Dinner, family time, and unwinding.

Be realistic about how long tasks take, and leave buffer time for transitions or unexpected interruptions.

Step 4: Build in Flexibility

While structure is important, life is unpredictable. Avoid overscheduling by leaving some open slots in your day for unforeseen events or spontaneous opportunities. Flexibility ensures that you can adapt without feeling overwhelmed.

Integrating Work, Rest, and Play

A fulfilling day includes a balance of productivity, rejuvenation, and enjoyment. Neglecting any of these areas can lead to stress, burnout, or a sense of emptiness. Let's break down how to integrate work, rest, and play into your schedule.

Work: Maximize Productivity

Work is an essential part of life, but it shouldn't dominate your day. To work efficiently without overextending yourself:

- **Set clear goals:** Begin each work session with specific, achievable objectives.
- **Use focused time:** Adopt techniques like the Pomodoro Technique (25 minutes of work followed by a 5-minute break) to maintain concentration.
- **Avoid multitasking:** Focus on one task at a time to improve quality and reduce stress.

Remember, productivity isn't about doing more—it's about doing what matters.

Rest: Recharge Your Energy

Rest is not a luxury; it's a necessity. Without adequate rest, your productivity, health, and mood will suffer. Here's how to incorporate rest into your day:

- **Schedule breaks:** Take short breaks every hour and longer breaks between work blocks to recharge.
- **Practice mindfulness:** Use meditation, deep breathing, or stretching to calm your mind and reset.
- **Prioritize sleep:** Create a consistent bedtime routine that ensures you get enough restful sleep. Disconnect from screens at least an hour before bed and engage in calming activities like reading or journaling.

Rest isn't just about physical downtime—it's also about mental and emotional renewal.

Play: Cultivate Joy

Play adds fun and creativity to your life, making your days more enjoyable and fulfilling. Play doesn't have to be elaborate; it simply needs to bring you joy. Examples include:

- **Hobbies:** Engage in activities like painting, gardening, cooking, or playing an instrument.
- **Social time:** Spend time with loved ones, share laughs, and build connections.
- **Physical activity:** Choose exercises or sports that you genuinely enjoy, such as dancing, hiking, or yoga.

Even small moments of play can have a big impact on your mood and energy.

Putting It All Together

Designing your perfect day involves blending work, rest, and play into a seamless flow that feels natural and fulfilling. Here's an example of a balanced daily schedule:

- **7:00 AM:** Morning routine (stretching, meditation, light breakfast)
- **8:00 AM:** Exercise (a brisk walk or yoga session)
- **9:00 AM:** Focused work on top-priority tasks
- **12:00 PM:** Lunch and a 20-minute walk
- **1:00 PM:** Collaborative tasks or meetings
- **3:30 PM:** Short break with a fun activity (listen to music, play a game)
- **4:00 PM:** Finish workday with low-energy tasks
- **6:00 PM:** Dinner with family or friends
- **7:00 PM:** Personal time for hobbies or relaxation
- **9:00 PM:** Wind-down routine (journaling, reading, gratitude practice)
- **10:00 PM:** Bedtime

Tailor this template to suit your lifestyle, values, and responsibilities.

The Benefits of a Well-Designed Day

When you design your day with intention, you'll experience profound benefits:

- **Improved focus and efficiency:** A clear structure eliminates decision fatigue and allows you to concentrate on what matters.
- **Enhanced well-being:** Balancing work with rest and play prevents burnout and promotes overall health.
- **Deeper satisfaction:** Spending time on meaningful activities creates a sense of purpose and fulfillment.
- **Greater flexibility:** A well-planned day is resilient, allowing you to adapt to life's surprises without losing balance.

Designing your perfect day is a dynamic process. As your priorities and circumstances change, so should your schedule. Periodically review and adjust your plan to ensure it continues to serve your goals and needs.

Chapter 4: Saying No Without Guilt

One of the most powerful tools for reclaiming your time and living intentionally is the ability to say "no" without guilt. Yet, many people struggle with this simple word, fearing conflict, rejection, or the burden of disappointing others. Mastering the art of refusal is essential for prioritizing what truly matters, protecting your energy, and maintaining balance in your life. In this chapter, we'll explore practical strategies for saying no confidently and gracefully while staying focused on your core values and goals.

How to Master the Art of Refusal

Saying no is an act of self-respect and self-care, but it requires practice and a shift in mindset. The following steps will help you refine this skill so that you can set boundaries and protect your time.

Step 1: Understand Your Hesitation

To say no effectively, it's important to understand why it feels so difficult. Common reasons include:

- **Fear of disappointing others:** You don't want to let someone down or risk damaging a relationship.
- **Desire for approval:** You want to be liked or seen as helpful.
- **Guilt:** You feel obligated to help, even if it comes at your own expense.

Acknowledging these feelings is the first step toward overcoming them. Remember, saying no doesn't make you selfish or unkind—it makes you intentional and respectful of your limits.

Step 2: Reframe Your Perspective

Shift how you view the act of saying no:

- **It's about priorities:** Saying no to one thing means saying yes to something more important. It's not rejection; it's redirection.
- **It builds respect:** Setting boundaries shows others that you value your time and expect the same respect from them.
- **It strengthens relationships:** By setting clear expectations, you avoid overcommitting and feeling resentful, leading to healthier interactions.

This mindset shift helps you see refusal as an act of empowerment, not conflict.

Step 3: Use Clear and Polite Language

When declining a request, clarity and kindness go a long way. Here are some examples of how to say no in various situations:

- **Direct but polite:** "Thank you for thinking of me, but I'm unable to take this on right now."
- **Deferring:** "I can't commit to this at the moment, but I'd be happy to revisit it in the future."
- **Offering alternatives:** "I'm not the best person for this, but [Name] might be able to help."
- **Prioritizing:** "I wish I could, but my schedule is full with higher-priority commitments."

Avoid overexplaining or making excuses. A simple and honest response is often enough.

Step 4: Practice Assertiveness

Being assertive doesn't mean being rude or aggressive; it means standing firm in your decision. Use confident body language and a calm tone when saying no. For example:

- Make eye contact.
- Speak slowly and deliberately.
- Avoid using uncertain phrases like "I think" or "maybe."

Assertiveness conveys that your decision is final and not open to negotiation.

Step 5: Role-Play and Reflect

If you're new to saying no, practice with a trusted friend or in front of a mirror. Role-playing different scenarios can help you feel more confident in real-life situations. Afterward, reflect on how it felt and adjust your approach as needed.

Focusing on What Truly Matters

Saying no is only effective when it's rooted in a clear understanding of your priorities. To focus on what truly matters, you must first define what those priorities are and align your actions with them.

Step 1: Clarify Your Values and Goals

Your values and goals act as a compass, guiding your decisions. Ask yourself:

- What are my core values (e.g., family, health, career, creativity)?
- What are my short-term and long-term goals?
- What activities or commitments bring me the most joy and fulfillment?

Write these down and refer to them whenever you're faced with a new request or opportunity.

Step 2: Create a Priority Filter

A priority filter is a mental checklist that helps you evaluate whether to say yes or no to a request. Use questions like:

- Does this align with my values?
- Will it help me achieve my goals?
- Do I have the time and energy for this without compromising my well-being?
- What am I giving up by saying yes to this?

If the answer to most of these questions is no, then saying no is the right choice.

Step 3: Limit Your Obligations

Overcommitting dilutes your focus and drains your energy. Be intentional about the number of commitments you take on:

- **Set a maximum:** For example, limit yourself to one major project at a time or two social outings per week.
- **Decline recurring obligations:** If a weekly meeting or event no longer serves you, step away from it.

By reducing your obligations, you create space for the things that truly matter.

Step 4: Protect Your "Yes"

Every time you say yes, you're making a commitment. Treat your yes as a valuable resource:

- **Delay your response:** If you're unsure, ask for time to think: "Let me check my schedule and get back to you."
- **Prioritize your time:** Reserve your yes for opportunities that excite you or align with your goals.
- **Set clear expectations:** If you do say yes, be clear about what you can and cannot do.

Protecting your yes ensures that your time and energy are used wisely.

Overcoming Guilt and External Pressure

Even with practice, saying no can still trigger feelings of guilt or pressure from others. Here's how to manage these challenges:

Reframe Guilt as Growth

Guilt often stems from a desire to please others. Instead of viewing it as a negative emotion, see it as a sign that you're growing and setting healthy boundaries. Remind yourself:

- Saying no is a form of self-respect.
- You're modeling healthy behavior for others.
- Every no is an opportunity to focus on what truly matters.

Respond to Pressure with Grace

Sometimes, others may push back when you say no. Stay calm and assertive:

- **Restate your decision:** "I understand this is important to you, but I really can't take it on right now."
- **Offer empathy:** "I wish I could help, but I need to focus on my current commitments."
- **Stand firm:** Repeat your response if necessary, without wavering.

Remember, their reaction is about them, not you.

The Benefits of Saying No

Mastering the art of refusal has transformative effects on your life:

- **More time and energy:** You free yourself from unnecessary obligations, creating space for what truly matters.
- **Greater focus:** By prioritizing your goals, you can direct your efforts toward meaningful pursuits.
- **Improved relationships:** Setting boundaries reduces resentment and fosters mutual respect.
- **Enhanced well-being:** Protecting your time and energy leads to lower stress and greater fulfillment.

Saying no isn't about rejection—it's about intention. It's about choosing a life that aligns with your values, respects your boundaries, and honors your time. As you embrace this skill, you'll find that your days become more focused, balanced, and deeply rewarding.

Chapter 5: Living with Intent

Intentional living is the cornerstone of a meaningful life. It's about aligning your time and energy with your values, ensuring that every action, decision, and commitment serves a purpose. When you live with intent, you create a life that feels authentic, fulfilling, and aligned with your deepest priorities. This chapter explores how to align your time with your values and sustain a minimalist mindset to maintain clarity and focus.

Aligning Time with Your Values

Your values act as a compass, guiding your decisions and shaping your life. However, in the chaos of modern living, it's easy to lose sight of these values and fall into patterns that don't reflect what truly matters. By intentionally aligning your time with your values, you can create a life that feels balanced and purposeful.

Step 1: Identify Your Core Values

Core values are the principles that matter most to you. They are the foundation of your identity and the key to understanding what drives your happiness and fulfillment. To uncover your core values, ask yourself:

- What brings me the most joy and satisfaction?
- When do I feel most at peace or in flow?
- What do I want to be remembered for?

Common values include family, health, creativity, growth, freedom, service, and integrity. Take time to reflect and write down your top five values.

Step 2: Evaluate Your Current Commitments

Once you've identified your values, evaluate how your time is currently spent. Refer to your time audit from earlier chapters and ask:

- Which activities align with my values?
- Which commitments feel out of sync with what I care about?
- Where am I spending time out of obligation rather than intention?

Highlight areas where your time and values are mismatched, as these are opportunities for realignment.

Step 3: Create a Value-Based Schedule

Design your day, week, or month around your values. For each of your core values, list activities or habits that reflect them. Then, intentionally allocate time for these priorities:

- If family is a core value, schedule regular family dinners or outings.
- If health is important, dedicate time for exercise, meal prep, and self-care.
- If creativity matters, carve out time for hobbies, writing, or art.

Use tools like time-blocking or a digital calendar to ensure these activities are non-negotiable parts of your routine.

Step 4: Regularly Reflect and Adjust

Life evolves, and so do your priorities. Schedule regular check-ins—monthly or quarterly—to assess whether your time is still aligned with your values. Adjust as needed to accommodate changes in your goals or circumstances.

Sustaining a Minimalist Mindset

A minimalist mindset is not about deprivation but about intentionality. It's about stripping away the excess to focus on what truly matters. By sustaining a minimalist mindset, you can reduce stress, gain clarity, and create space for joy and meaning.

Step 1: Simplify Your Environment

Physical clutter can contribute to mental clutter. Begin by decluttering your space:

- **Start small:** Tackle one drawer, shelf, or room at a time.
- **Use the "joy test":** Keep only items that serve a purpose or bring you joy.
- **Adopt a "one in, one out" rule:** For every new item you bring into your space, remove one you no longer need.

A simplified environment fosters a sense of calm and focus, making it easier to live with intent.

Step 2: Streamline Your Digital Life

Digital clutter can be just as overwhelming as physical clutter. Take steps to simplify your digital environment:

- **Unsubscribe:** Remove yourself from unnecessary emails, newsletters, or notifications.
- **Organize files:** Create a system for storing and accessing digital documents, photos, and notes.
- **Limit screen time:** Set boundaries for social media, news, or entertainment apps to reduce distractions.

By decluttering your digital world, you free up mental space for more meaningful pursuits.

Step 3: Prioritize Quality Over Quantity

A minimalist mindset values depth and quality over volume and excess. This principle applies to all areas of life:

- **Relationships:** Nurture a few meaningful connections rather than spreading yourself thin.
- **Possessions:** Invest in fewer, high-quality items that last and bring satisfaction.
- **Experiences:** Focus on creating memorable moments rather than chasing endless activities.

By choosing quality over quantity, you ensure that your life is rich with meaning rather than filled with noise.

Step 4: Adopt a "Less Is More" Philosophy

Minimalism extends beyond material possessions. It's a way of approaching life with simplicity and focus:

- **Say no to excess commitments:** Protect your time by avoiding overcommitment.
- **Focus on essential goals:** Pursue fewer goals with greater dedication and impact.
- **Embrace stillness:** Allow yourself moments of quiet and rest to recharge and reflect.

A "less is more" philosophy encourages you to be intentional in every aspect of your life.

The Benefits of Intentional, Minimalist Living

When you align your time with your values and adopt a minimalist mindset, you unlock profound benefits:

- **Greater clarity:** With less clutter—physical, mental, or emotional—you can focus on what truly matters.
- **Reduced stress:** Eliminating unnecessary obligations and possessions creates a sense of peace.
- **Deeper fulfillment:** Spending time on activities that align with your values brings a sense of purpose and joy.
- **Improved relationships:** Intentional living fosters meaningful connections with loved ones.

Intentionality and minimalism are not about perfection; they're about creating a life that feels authentic and aligned with your goals. By living with intent, you reclaim control over your time and energy, ensuring that your days are filled with meaning and purpose.

Appendix A: Time-Saving Tools and Strategies

Efficient time management is key to living a meaningful and intentional life. To help you optimize your daily routine, this appendix provides a comprehensive list of tools, techniques, and strategies designed to save time and increase productivity. Whether you're managing work, personal commitments, or leisure activities, these resources can help you make the most of every moment.

1. Time-Tracking Tools

Time-tracking tools help you monitor how you spend your day, identify inefficiencies, and make data-driven adjustments. These tools are especially useful for conducting time audits or staying accountable to your schedule.

- **RescueTime**: Automatically tracks time spent on apps and websites, providing insights into productivity levels.
- **Toggl Track**: A simple tool for tracking time on tasks, ideal for freelancers or project-based work.
- **Clockify**: A free time-tracking app that allows for manual entry and detailed reporting.
- **Timely**: Uses AI to automatically track your activities and create accurate timesheets.

2. Calendar and Scheduling Tools

A well-maintained calendar is essential for managing commitments and ensuring balance in your life. These tools help you plan, organize, and protect your time.

- **Google Calendar**: A versatile, user-friendly calendar with scheduling, reminders, and event-sharing features.
- **Microsoft Outlook Calendar**: Integrates seamlessly with email and task management for business users.
- **Calendly**: Simplifies scheduling by allowing others to book time with you based on your availability.
- **TimeTree**: A shared calendar tool perfect for coordinating schedules with family or teams.

3. Task and Project Management Tools

Keeping track of tasks and projects is crucial for staying organized and productive. These tools can help you prioritize, delegate, and complete tasks efficiently.

- **Trello**: A visual project management tool using boards and cards for easy organization.
- **Asana**: Offers task assignments, timelines, and integrations for teams and individuals.
- **Notion**: Combines note-taking, task management, and project tracking in one customizable platform.
- **Todoist**: A simple and intuitive app for managing personal and professional to-do lists.

4. Automation Tools

Automation tools save time by handling repetitive tasks and streamlining workflows. They can be used for everything from email management to home automation.

- **Zapier**: Connects apps and automates workflows without coding.
- **IFTTT (If This Then That)**: Automates simple tasks, such as syncing calendars or sending reminders.
- **SaneBox**: Organizes your email inbox by filtering important messages and deferring unimportant ones.
- **Roomba or Roborock**: Robotic vacuums that save time on cleaning.

5. Communication and Collaboration Tools

Efficient communication tools reduce the back-and-forth often associated with emails or meetings, freeing up time for deep work.

- **Slack**: A messaging platform for teams that supports real-time collaboration and file sharing.
- **Zoom**: A video conferencing tool for remote meetings and webinars.
- **Microsoft Teams**: Combines chat, video calls, and file sharing for workplace collaboration.
- **Google Workspace**: Offers collaborative tools like Google Docs, Sheets, and Slides for real-time editing.

6. Digital Decluttering and Focus Tools

Digital distractions can be a significant time drain. These tools help you stay focused and minimize interruptions.

- **Freedom**: Blocks distracting websites and apps to improve focus.
- **Focus@Will**: Provides background music scientifically designed to enhance concentration.
- **Forest**: Encourages focus by growing a virtual tree when you stay off your phone.
- **OneTab**: Consolidates browser tabs into a single list, reducing clutter and improving focus.

7. Productivity Techniques

These time-tested strategies can help you work more efficiently and make better use of your time.

- **Pomodoro Technique**: Work in 25-minute intervals followed by 5-minute breaks to maintain focus and avoid burnout.
- **Eisenhower Matrix**: Prioritize tasks based on urgency and importance, focusing on high-value activities.
- **Time Blocking**: Allocate specific time slots for different activities to create structure in your day.
- **Batch Processing**: Group similar tasks together to minimize context switching (e.g., responding to emails or meal prepping).

8. Household Management Tools

Streamlining household tasks can save hours each week, giving you more time for what matters most.

- **Meal Planning Apps**: Apps like Mealime, Yummly, or Plan to Eat help you plan meals, generate grocery lists, and save time cooking.
- **Grocery Delivery Services**: Services like Instacart, Amazon Fresh, or Walmart+ save time by delivering groceries to your door.
- **Smart Home Devices**: Tools like Amazon Echo, Google Nest, or smart plugs can automate lighting, thermostats, and appliances.
- **Laundry Services**: Drop-off or pick-up laundry services can free up hours in your schedule.

9. Self-Care and Wellness Tools

Prioritizing self-care ensures you have the energy and focus to tackle your day effectively. These tools help you streamline wellness routines.

- **Headspace**: A guided meditation app for mindfulness and relaxation.
- **MyFitnessPal**: Tracks meals, workouts, and health goals.
- **Sleep Cycle**: Monitors sleep patterns and wakes you during your lightest sleep phase for better mornings.
- **Fitbit or Apple Watch**: Tracks fitness, sleep, and activity levels to promote a balanced lifestyle.

10. Time-Saving Life Hacks

In addition to tools, these practical strategies can shave minutes (or hours) off your day:

- **Prepare the night before:** Lay out clothes, pack lunches, and organize essentials to streamline your morning routine.
- **Use commute time wisely:** Listen to audiobooks, podcasts, or guided meditations while traveling.
- **Adopt a minimalist wardrobe:** Reduce decision fatigue by limiting clothing choices to versatile, high-quality pieces.
- **Keep essentials in stock:** Use subscription services for household staples to avoid last-minute store trips.

Bringing It All Together

Incorporating time-saving tools and strategies into your daily life doesn't require a complete overhaul—start with small changes and gradually build habits that align with your goals. By leveraging the resources in this appendix, you can optimize your time, reduce stress, and create space for what truly matters. Remember, the ultimate goal of time-saving is not just to do more but to live more meaningfully and intentionally.

<u>Message from the Author:</u>

I hope you enjoyed this book, I love astrology and knew there was not a book such as this out on the shelf. I love metaphysical items as well. Please check out my other books:

-Life of Government Benefits

-My life of Hell

-My life with Hydrocephalus

-Red Sky

-World Domination:Woman's rule

-World Domination:Woman's Rule 2: The War

-Life and Banishment of Apophis: book 1

-The Kidney Friendly Diet

-The Ultimate Hemp Cookbook

-Creating a Dispensary(legally)

-Cleanliness throughout life: the importance of showering from childhood to adulthood.

-Strong Roots: The Risks of Overcoddling children

-Hemp Horoscopes: Cosmic Insights and Earthly Healing

- Celestial Hemp Navigating the Zodiac: Through the Green Cosmos

-Astrological Hemp: Aligning The Stars with Earth's Ancient Herb

-The Astrological Guide to Hemp: Stars, Signs, and Sacred Leaves

-Green Growth: Innovative Marketing Strategies for your Hemp Products and Dispensary

-Cosmic Cannabis

-Astrological Munchies

-Henry The Hemp

-Zodiacal Roots: The Astrological Soul Of Hemp

- **Green Constellations: Intersection of Hemp and Zodiac**

-Hemp in The Houses: An astrological Adventure Through The Cannabis Galaxy

-Galactic Ganja Guide

Heavenly Hemp

Zodiac Leaves

Doctor Who Astrology

Cannastrology

Stellar Satvias and Cosmic Indicas

Celestial Cannabis: A Zodiac Journey

AstroHerbology: The Sky and The Soil: Volume 1

AstroHerbology:Celestial Cannabis:Volume 2

Cosmic Cannabis Cultivation

The Starry Guide to Herbal Harmony: Volume 1

The Starry Guide to Herbal Harmony: Cannabis Universe: Volume 2

Yugioh Astrology: Astrological Guide to Deck, Duels and more

Nightmare Mansion: Echoes of The Abyss

Nightmare Mansion 2: Legacy of Shadows

Nightmare Mansion 3: Shadows of the Forgotten

Nightmare Mansion 4: Echoes of the Damned

The Life and Banishment of Apophis: Book 2

Nightmare Mansion: Halls of Despair

Healing with Herb: Cannabis and Hydrocephalus

Planetary Pot: Aligning with Astrological Herbs: Volume 1

Fast Track to Freedom: 30 Days to Financial Independence Using AI, Assets, and Agile Hustles

Cosmic Hemp Pathways

How to Become Financially Free in 30 Days: 10,000 Paths to Prosperity

Zodiacal Herbage: Astrological Insights: Volume 1

Nightmare Mansion: Whispers in the Walls

The Daleks Invade Atlantis

Henry the hemp and Hydrocephalus

10X The Kidney Friendly Diet

Cannabis Universe: Adult coloring book

Hemp Astrology: The Healing Power of the Stars

Zodiacal Herbage: Astrological Insights: Cannabis Universe: Volume 2

<u>Planetary Pot: Aligning with Astrological Herbs: Cannabis Universes: Volume 2</u>

Doctor Who Meets the Replicators and SG-1: The Ultimate Battle for Survival

Nightmare Mansion: Curse of the Blood Moon

<u>The Celestial Stoner: A Guide to the Zodiac</u>

Cosmic Pleasures: Sex Toy Astrology for Every Sign

Hydrocephalus Astrology: Navigating the Stars and Healing Waters

Lapis and the Mischievous Chocolate Bar

Celestial Positions: Sexual Astrology for Every Sign

Apophis's Shadow Work Journal: : A Journey of Self-Discovery and Healing

Kinky Cosmos: Sexual Kink Astrology for Every Sign

Digital Cosmos: The Astrological Digimon Compendium

Stellar Seeds: The Cosmic Guide to Growing with Astrology

Apophis's Daily Gratitude Journal

Cat Astrology: Feline Mysteries of the Cosmos

The Cosmic Kama Sutra: An Astrological Guide to Sexual Positions

Unleash Your Potential: A Guided Journal Powered by AI Insights

Whispers of the Enchanted Grove

Cosmic Pleasures: An Astrological Guide to Sexual Kinks

369, 12 Manifestation Journal

Whisper of the nocturne journal(blank journal for writing or drawing)

The Boogey Book

Locked In Reflection: A Chastity Journey Through Locktober

Generating Wealth Quickly:

How to Generate $100,000 in 24 Hours

Star Magic: Harness the Power of the Universe

The Flatulence Chronicles: A Fart Journal for Self-Discovery

The Doctor and The Death Moth

Seize the Day: A Personal Seizure Tracking Journal

The Ultimate Boogeyman Safari: A Journey into the Boogie World and Beyond

Whispers of Samhain: 1,000 Spells of Love, Luck, and Lunar Magic: Samhain Spell Book

Apophis's guides:

Witch's Spellbook Crafting Guide for Halloween

<u>Frost & Flame: The Enchanted Yule Grimoire of 1000 Winter Spells</u>

<u>The Ultimate Boogey Goo Guide & Spooky Activities for Halloween Fun</u>

Harmony of the Scales: A Libra's Spellcraft for Balance and Beauty

The Enchanted Advent: 36 Days of Christmas Wonders

Nightmare Mansion: The Labyrinth of Screams

Harvest of Enchantment: 1,000 Spells of Gratitude, Love, and Fortune for Thanksgiving

The Boogey Chronicles: A Journal of Nightly Encounters and Shadowy Secrets

The 12 Days of Financial Freedom: A Step-by-Step Christmas Countdown to Transform Your Finances

Sigil of the Eternal Spiral Blank Journal

A Christmas Feast: Timeless Recipes for Every Meal

Cosmic Sales: The Astrological Guide to Black Friday Shopping

Legends of the Corn Mother and Other Harvest Myths

Whispers of the Harvest: The Corn Mother's Journal

The Evergreen Spellbook

The Doctor Meets the Boogeyman

The White Witch of Rose Hall's SpellBook

The Gingerbread Golem's Shadow: A Study in Sweet Darkness

The Gingerbread Golem Codex: An Academic Exploration of Sweet Myths

The Gingerbread Golem Grimoire: Sweet Magicks and Spells for the Festive Witch

The Curse of the Gingerbread Golem

10-minute Christmas Crafts for kids

<u>Christmas Crisis Solutions: The Ultimate Last-Minute Survival Guide</u>

Gingerbread Golem Recipes: Holiday Treats with a Magical Twist

The Infinite Key: Unlocking Mystical Secrets of the Ages

Enchanted Yule: A Wiccan and Pagan Guide to a Magical and Memorable Season

Dinosaurs of Power: Unlocking Ancient Magick

Astro-Dinos: The Cosmic Guide to Prehistoric Wisdom

Gallifrey's Yule Logs: A Festive Doctor Who Cookbook

The Dino Grimoire: Secrets of Prehistoric Magick

The Gift They Never Knew They Needed

The Gingerbread Golem's Culinary Alchemy: Enchanting Recipes for a Sweetly Dark Feast

A Time Lord Christmas: Holiday Adventures with the Doctor

Krampusproofing Your Home: Defensive Strategies for Yule

Silent Frights: A Collection of Christmas Creepypastas to Chill Your Bones

Santa Raptor's Jolly Carnage: A Dino-Claus Christmas Tale

Prehistoric Palettes: A Dino Wicca Coloring Journey

The Christmas Wishkeeper Chronicles

The Starlight Sleigh: A Holiday Journey

Elf Secrets: The True Magic of the North Pole

Candy Cane Conjurations

Cooking with Kids: Recipes Under 20 Minutes

Doctor Who: The TARDIS Confiscation

The Anxiety First Aid Kit: Quick Tools to Calm Your Mind

Frosty Whispers: A Winter's Tale

The Infinite Key: Unlocking the Secrets to Prosperity, Resilience, and Purpose

The Grasping Void: Why You'll Regret This Purchase

Astrology for Busy Bees: Star Signs Simplified

The Instant Focus Formula: Cut Through the Noise

The Secret Language of Colors: Unlocking the Emotional Codes

Sacred Fossil Chronicles: Blank Journal

The Christmas Cottage Miracle

Feeding Frenzy: Graboid-Inspired Recipes

Manifest in Minutes: The Quick Law of Attraction Guide

The Symbiote Chronicles: Doctor Who's Venomous Journey

Think Tiny, Grow Big: The Minimalist Mindset

The Energy Key: Unlocking Limitless Motivation

New Year, New Magic: Manifesting Your Best Year Yet

Unstoppable You: Mastering Confidence in Minutes

Infinite Energy: The Secret to Never Feeling Drained

Lightning Focus: Mastering the Art of Productivity in a Distracted World

Saturnalia Manifestation Magick: A Guide to Unlocking Abundance During the Solstice

Graboids and Garland: The Ultimate Tremors-Themed Christmas Guide

12 Nights of Holiday Magic

The Power of Pause: 60-Second Mindfulness Practices

The Quick Reset: How to Reclaim Your Life After Burnout

The Shadow Eater: A Tale of Despair and Survival

The Micro-Mastery Method: Transform Your Skills in Just Minutes a Day

If you want solar for your home go here: https://www.harborsolar.live/apophisenterprises/

Get Some Tarot cards: https://www.makeplayingcards.com/sell/apophis-occult-shop

<u>Get some shirts: https://www.bonfire.com/store/apophis-shirt-emporium/</u>

<u>**Instagrams:**</u>
@apophis_enterprises,
@apophisbookemporium,
@apophisscardshop
Twitter: @apophisenterpr1
Tiktok:@apophisenterprise
Youtube: @sg1fan23477, @FiresideRetreatKingdom
Hive: @sg1fan23477
CheeLee: @SG1fan23477

Podcast: Apophis Chat Zone: https://open.spotify.com/show/5zXbrCLEV2xzCp8ybrfHsk?si=fb4d4fdbdce44dec

Newsletter: https://apophiss-newsletter-27c897.beehiiv.com/

If you want to support me or see posts of other projects that I have come over to: **buymeacoffee.com/mpetchinskg**
I post there daily several times a day

Get your Dinowicca or Christmas themed digital products, especially Santa Raptor songs and other musics. Here:
https://sg1fan23477.gumroad.com

Apophis Yuletide Digital has not only digital Christmas items, but it will have all things with Dinowicca as well as other Digital products.

www.ingramcontent.com/pod-product-compliance
Lightning Source LLC
Chambersburg PA
CBHW072127150726
47999CB00005B/2165